CLAIMING OUR RIGHTS

BY

E.W. KENYON

CROSSREACH PUBLICATIONS

Hope. Inspiration. Trust.

CONTENTS

CHRISTIANITY IS A LEGAL DOCUMENT

Most of our basic legal terminology comes from the Scripture. The very titles, Old Covenant and New Covenant, are legal terms. Every step in the plan of Redemption, from the Fall of Man until Jesus Christ was seated at the right hand of the Majesty on High, having redeemed the human race, is simply a series of legal steps perfecting the most remarkable Legal Document the human has in its possession.

The plan of Redemption cannot he understood unless one reads it from the legal point of view. In this plan of Redemption there are three parties to the contract: God, Man, and Satan. God must be just to Himself, just to Man, and just to the Devil.

We understand that God created man, placing him here on the earth, and that He conferred upon him certain legal rights. Legal rights that are conferred are more easily forfeited than those that come by nature. These rights man transferred to Satan, God's enemy. This brings the Devil into the plan so that he must be dealt with, and the whole scheme of Redemption is God's seeking to redeem the human race from Adam's sin, and doing it upon such an equitable basis that it will perfectly satisfy the claims of Justice, meet the needs of man, and defeat Satan on legal grounds.

The Fall of Man was a lawful act; that is, Adam had legal right to transfer the authority and dominion that God had placed in his hands into the hands of another. This gives Satan a legal right to rule over man and over creation.

The plan of Redemption is one of the most ingenious and most wonderful of all the many works of God. Notice what He is obliged to do. Man sold himself out to the Devil, making himself a bond slave, and that slavery will last until the lease or period of man's dominion expires. God must in some way redeem fallen man from his sin, and Satan's dominion. He must do it in such a way as not to be unjust to Satan, nor unjust to man. God must recognize and hold inviolate man's treacherous act of transference of dominion. It was a legal act, and God has no right to arbitrarily annul it. He must show to Satan perfect justice at all points, and at the same time He must reach man in his helplessness and redeem him.

In order to do this, it is necessary that one come to the earth who is not a subject of Satan, and yet a man, and as a man meet every demand of justice against man. In order to accomplish this, there must be an Incarnation. This Incarnate one must not be a subject of Satan, nor a subject of death, and to this end God sends the Holy Spirit to a virgin in Judah, and she conceives and bears a son. This son is born, not of natural generation but of supernatural. The child is not a subject of death nor of Satan. He has the same type of a body that the first man, Adam, had before he sinned. Every step of the work that was accomplished by this Incarnate One was based upon perfectly legal grounds.

This Incarnate One met the demands, first, of the heart of Deity for a perfect human who would do His will; second, He met the demands of fallen man in that as a man He met the Devil and conquered him in honorable open combat. "Being tempted in all points, yet without sin." He goes on the Cross, and God lays upon him the iniquity of the human race. He, then, with this burden upon Him and under Judgment of God, goes down into Hell and suffers the penalty demanded by Justice.

When He had paid this penalty, He arose from the dead. He conquered Satan. He broke his dominion and took away his authority and power. Then, with the trophies of His triumph, He ascended to the right band of the Majesty on High and laid the tokens of His victory at the feet of His Great Father.

On the ground of this victory, the sinner has a legal right to accept Jesus Christ as a personal Savior. He has a legal right to Eternal Life. He has a legal right to Victory over sin and Satan. He has a legal right to a home in Heaven. He has a legal right to use the Name of Jesus in prayer. He has a legal right to his Father's protection and care. He has a legal right to a son's place in the Family of God. He has a legal right to the indwelling presence of the Holy Spirit, to the care and protection of the Spirit, and to the intercession and teaching of the Spirit. He has a legal right to be translated at the Second Coming of the Lord Jesus. He has a legal right to immortality for the body. He has a legal right to an inheritance in the New Heavens and New Earth. He has a legal right to live with his Father throughout Eternity.

Are We Claiming Our Rights?

There is no excuse for the spiritual weakness and poverty of the Family of God when the wealth of Grace and Love of our great Father with His power and wisdom are all at our disposal. We are not coming to the Father as a tramp coming to the door begging for food; we come as sons not only claiming our legal rights but claiming the natural rights of a child that is begotten in love. No one can hinder us or question our right of approach to our Father.

When we realize the great need of the unsaved world and know that need can only be met by the great heart of the Father operating through the Church, it stirs us to mighty intercession for a needy world. God cannot touch the human today except through the Church. It is His only mediator, and if the Church fails to assume its obligation then the hand of God is powerless. It staggers one to realize that God has limited Himself to our prayer life, and when we refuse to assume the obligations of prayer, God's hands are paralyzed.

OUR AUTHORITY

"For sin shall not have dominion over you: for ye are not under law, but under grace" (*Romans 6:14*), or "Sin shall not Lord it over you. Sin has lost its dominion or authority over us. Satan has no legal authority over the New Creation, though he has over the old.

Satan has Legal Rights over the sinner that God cannot dispute or challenge. He can sell them as slaves; he owns them, body, soul and spirit. But the moment we are born again... receive Eternal Life, the nature of God,—his legal dominion ends.

Christ is the Legal Head of the New Creation, or Family of God, and all the Authority that was given Him, He has given us: (Matthew 28:18), "All authority in heaven," the seat of authority, and "on earth," the place of execution of authority. He is "head over all things," the highest authority in the Universe, for the benefit of the Church which is His body.

Ephesians 1:20, "Which he wrought in Christ, when he raised him from the dead, and set him at his own right hand in the heavenly places." Here He is at the "Right Hand of God." "Far above," that is, His seat of authority transcends all other rulers.

Philippians 2:9-11, "Wherefore also God highly exalted him, and gave unto him the name which is above every name that in the name of Jesus every knee should bow, of things in heaven and things on earth and things under the earth, and that every tongue should confess that Jesus Christ is Lord, to the glory of God the Father." He has the Name above every name in the three worlds: Heaven, Earth, and Hell.

Every demon and angel is subject to the Imperial Name of Jesus and, wonder of wonders, He gave us the Power of Attorney to use that Name of Might. All our Authority is based on His Finished Work, but it is all enwrapped in His name. By His giving us the Legal use of this name He has put omnipotence at our disposal in our combat with Satanic hosts.

Mark 16:17-20, "And these signs shall accompany them that believe: in my name shall they cast out demons; they shall speak with new tongues; they shall take up serpents, and if they drink any deadly thing, it shall in no wise hurt them; they shall lay hands on the sick, and they shall recover.

"So then the Lord Jesus, after he had spoken unto them, was received up into heaven and sat down at the right hand of God. And they went forth, and preached everywhere, the Lord working with them, and confirming the word by the signs that followed. In my name shall they cast out demons." Here He defines our Legal Authority.

We shall cast out demons: (this means Authority over demons in their relation to men;) cast them out of peoples' bodies; break their power over those bodies, minds, and spirits; break their power over meetings, homes, and sometimes communities. Our combat is not against flesh and blood but against the principalities, and powers in heavenly places; or in other words our war is against demons of all ranks, kinds, and authorities. They are attacking the human everywhere, and especially the children of God.

How are we to defend ourselves against them, or lead an assault on their hosts, and deliver the captives? The air is pregnant with evil spirits who seek to infest our bodies as bats do old buildings. The awful power of evil in our land eloquently proves what we write.

"In my Name ye shall speak in new tongues." This new and startling manifestation of the Spirit is our Legal Right in the Name, where all the mighty powers of God are kept for us.

"In my Name they shall take up serpents, and if they drink any deadly thing it shall not harm them. They shall lay hands on the sick, and they shall recover." Here it is not sufference or pity, but Legal Authority. You have as much right to demand healing as you have to demand the cashing of a check at a bank where you have a deposit. You have a Legal Right to deliverance from Satan.

If any one oppresses you or enslaves you in this country, you have a Legal Right to protection from the government to which you belong and pay taxes. So you have Legal Rights in the Family of God. No man has a right to hold a white slave today; neither has Satan a Legal Right to hold a child of God in bondage. All disease is of the Devil. How glad the Father would be, if we would arise and take our Legal Rights. All bad habits are of the Devil.

John 14:13-14, 15:16, 16:23-24, "And whatsoever ye shall ask in my name, that will I do, that the Father may be glorified in the Son. If ye shall ask anything in my name, that will I do."

This scripture does not refer to prayer as do the others. It is not coming to the Father with a petition, but it is taking the Master's place. It is using His authority to cast out demons, to heal the sick. A literal translation would read: "If ye shall demand anything in my name, that will I do." In His place we demand sickness and demons to leave in the authority of His Name, and He is there to confirm by His power the word that we speak. This scripture refers to our using the authority that He gave us in Mark 16:17-18.

Now notice John 16:23-24. "That whatsoever ye shall ask of the Father in my name, he will give it to you. And in that day ye shall ask me nothing. Verily, verily, I say unto you, If ye ask anything of the Father, he will give it you in my name. Hitherto have ye asked nothing in my name; ask, and ye shall receive, that your joy may be made full." This is praying to the Father in Jesus' Name.

Here the Mighty Son of God who is now seated in the highest seat of Authority in the Universe gives us the Legal Power of Attorney to use the Might, Authority, and Power of His Name, in our earth struggles against Satan and demons. In the face of this mighty Fact, poverty and weakness of spirit are criminal. Here all Heaven with its might and Authority are at our disposal.

It is not trying to have Faith, but knowing the Legal Rights that are yours, as much yours as the clothes you wear—as the bed you sleep on,—the hat you wear, all yours, legally, blessedly yours.

Satan cannot stand before that Name now, any more than he could before the Man who gave you the right to use it, when He walked in Galilee. Disease is as impotent before it now as it was when its owner, as the Son of Man, walked on earth. Demons fear it today in the lips of a person who walks with God, as when they bowed before it in Jesus' Day.

All Hell knows the power of that Name; they know our Legal Rights and Authority. So they are fighting to keep us in ignorance of our Legal Rights; or if we know them, to keep us under condemnation so we will not dare use them.

Matthew 18:18-20, "Verily I say unto you, what things soever ye shall bind on earth shall be bound in heaven; and what things soever ye shall loose on earth shall be loosed in heaven. Again I say unto you, that if two of you shall agree on earth as touching anything that they shall ask, it shall be done for them of my Father who is in Heaven. For where two or three are gathered together in my name, there am I in the midst of them." Here the heart stands hushed at its power and God-delegated Authority.

"Whatsoever ye shall bind on earth shall be bound in heaven." This is unexplored territory to most men today. We can bind Demons, bind disease, and habits, and bind men so they can not go on in the will of Satan; or use fearsome power to deliver souls over to Satan for the destruction of the body. "For I verily, being absent in body but present in spirit, have already as though I were present judged him that hath so wrought this thing, in the name of our Lord Jesus, we being gathered together, and my spirit, with power of our Lord Jesus, to deliver such a one unto Satan for the destruction of the Flesh, that the spirit may be saved in the day of Lord Jesus" (*I Corinthians 5:3-5*).

We may bind the power of Satan over a community, making it easy for men to accept Christ. "Whatsoever ye shall loose on earth shall be loosed in heaven." Whatever in Jesus' name we set free, God in Heaven will make good.

What power we have! Let's use it! Will we arise to our mighty, heaven-given privileges? Look at the bound men and women everywhere, and the Word challenges us to go out and set the prisoner free.

What does this mean? All that it says, thank God. You can set diseased men free. We are doing it daily in our work! You can set demon-bound men free; you can break the chains that bind men, in that mighty Name. Most Christians are bound in some manner, either in testimony or in prayer, by fear and devilish doubt; they can be set free by a word if we use that name and then take their privileges.

What bondage to the world, and the binding, devilish spirit of the age we endure, that unseen bondage of the god of this age. How he holds men in leash! Yet every spirit may be free, yes, as free as Jesus.

What bondage to the fear of man; yet one authoritative word and the bond shall be broken.

What bondage to fear of want that makes men give pennies instead of dollars; yet there is freedom, glorious freedom for every bondaged soul. Reader! the Spirit is challenging you to arise and live this Truth.

What prayer meetings we would have if the Christians were free in prayer and testimony! God's hands are tied until He can use ours. Angels are our servants. They cannot do our work. God is limited to our Faith, our obedience. God is as small in the world as we make Him. God is big only where some man makes Him big, by using this divinely given authority. We are the body of Christ; the Head is powerless without our hands and feet.

Oh, men, can't you see how helpless God is until we let Him live omnipotently in our acts? A sin in the heart binds the arms of God that would embrace a multitude. Our fear to be used binds God's omnipotence.

Men of God, be God's men and use the authority delegated to you.

How The Early Church Used Their Authority

The Book of Acts is largely our Text Book; it is a series of stories of the triumphs of the Name of Jesus.

The first recorded use of their new heaven conferred authority is given in the third chapter, the healing of the impotent man at the Beautiful Gate. How quietly and assuredly the apostles say, "In the Name of Jesus Christ of Nazareth, arise and walk.' How God responds, and the man is healed. How the city is again moved, how Judaism is shaken! The apostles are arrested, forbidden to use the Name or preach in it. That Name has power in it. Jesus did no greater miracles when on earth than are recorded in the Book of Acts as done through His Name.

We see Peter striking a man and woman dead for lying. Awful power this is; power to heal and power to slay. They were walking in the omnipotence of the authority given them by Jesus. They were taking the words of Jesus seriously. They were acting as though the Word of God was true.

We have not space to tell of the men who walked in the freshness of this grace of God. We see Paul cause blindness to come upon the opposers. We see him cast out demons from Mediums. We see him stung by a viper and no harm come. We see the sick healed, the dead raised. Whole heathen cities turn toward the unknown God of the Jews.

In thirty-three short years this gospel, backed by the power of the Name, in the hands of common men was carried into every part of the Roman World. We see aprons, handkerchiefs, touched by Paul, sent out and laid on the sick, do the same mighty acts that Paul did in person.

These men lived in bodies like ours, with passions like ours, made mistakes as we do; yet they wrought miracles by this God-inspired authority over demons and disease. They were just men of like passions with us. What ails us, why do we not walk in power instead of weakness?

Paul could deliver a man over unto Satan for destruction of his body, or as he did Hymeneus and Alexander, that they might be taught not to blaspheme (*I Timothy 1:20*)—"Of whom is Hymeneus and Alexander whom I delivered unto Satan, that they might be taught not to blaspheme."

Preachers were dangerous in those days. Christians had power to prove their claims. They preached; they practiced. They made good. "They delivered the goods," as men say today.

Their Faith stood not in word only, but in demonstration and power. Miracles were the common order of the day. Christianity was a miracle in their day.

ABOUT CROSSREACH PUBLICATIONS

Thank you for choosing CrossReach Publications.

Hope. Inspiration. Trust.

CROSSREACH PUBLICATIONS These three words sum up the philosophy of why CrossReach Publications exist. To create inspiration for the present thus inspiring hope for the future, through trusted authors from previous generations.

We are *non-denominational* and *non-sectarian*. We appreciate and respect what every part of the body brings to the table and believe everyone has the right to study and come to their own conclusions. We aim to help facilitate that end.

We aspire to excellence. If we have not met your standards, please contact us and let us know. We want you to feel satisfied with your product. Something for everyone. We publish quality books both in presentation and content from a wide variety of authors who span various doctrinal positions and traditions, on a wide variety of Christian topics that will teach, encourage, challenge, inspire and equip.

We're a family-based home-business. A husband and wife team raising 8 kids. If you have any questions or comments about our publications email us at:

ContactUs@CrossReach.net

Don't forget you can follow us on <u>Facebook</u> and <u>Twitter</u>, (links are on the copyright page above) to keep up to date on our newest titles and deals.

BESTSELLING TITLES FROM CROSSREACH[1]

How to Be Filled with the Holy Spirit
A. W. Tozer

Before we deal with the question of how to be filled with the Holy Spirit, there are some matters which first have to be settled. As believers you have to get them out of the way, and right here is where the difficulty arises. I have been afraid that my listeners might have gotten the idea somewhere that I had a how-to-be-filled-with-the-Spirit-in-five-easy-lessons doctrine, which I could give you. If you can have any such vague ideas as that, I can only stand before you and say, "I am sorry"; because it isn't true; I can't give you such a course. There are some things, I say, that you have to get out of the way, settled.

God Still Speaks
A. W. Tozer

Tozer is as popular today as when he was living on the earth. He is respected right across the spectrum of Christianity, in circles that would disagree sharply with him doctrinally. Why is this? A. W. Tozer was a man who knew the voice of God. He

---

[1] Buy from CrossReach Publications for quality and price. We have a full selection of titles in print and eBook. All available on Amazon and other online stores. You can see our full selection just by searching for CrossReach Publications in the search bar!

shared this experience with every true child of God. With all those who are called by the grace of God to share in the mystical union that is possible with Him through His Son Jesus.

Tozer fought against much dryness and formality in his day. Considered a mighty man of God by most Evangelicals today, he was unconventional in his approach to spirituality and had no qualms about consulting everyone from Catholic Saints to German Protestant mystics for inspiration on how to experience God more fully.

Tozer, just like his Master, doesn't fit neatly into our theological boxes. He was a man after God's own heart and was willing to break the rules (man-made ones that is) to get there.

Here are two writings by Tozer that touch on the heart of this goal. Revelation is Not Enough and The Speaking Voice. A bonus chapter The Menace of the Religious Movie is included.

This is meat to sink your spiritual teeth into. Tozer's writings will show you the way to satisfy your spiritual hunger.

WHAT WE ARE IN CHRIST

What We Are in Christ
E. W. Kenyon

I was surprised to find that the expressions "in Christ," "in whom," and "in Him" occur more than 130 times in the New Testament. This is the heart of the Revelation of Redemption given to Paul.

Here is the secret of faith—faith that conquers, faith that moves mountains. Here is the secret of the Spirit's guiding us into all reality. The heart craves intimacy with the Lord Jesus and with the Father. This craving can now be satisfied.

Ephesians 1:7: "In whom we have our redemption through his blood, the remission of our trespasses according to the riches of his grace."

It is not a beggarly Redemption, but a real liberty in Christ that we have now. It is a Redemption by the God Who could say, "Let there be lights in the firmament of heaven," and cause the whole starry heavens to leap into being in a single instant. It is Omnipotence beyond human reason. This is where philosophy has never left a footprint.

Claiming Our Rights
E. W. Kenyon

CLAIMING OUR RIGHTS

E. W. KENYON

There is no excuse for the spiritual weakness and poverty of the Family of God when the wealth of Grace and Love of our great Father with His power and wisdom are all at our disposal. We are not coming to the Father as a tramp coming to the door begging for food; we come as sons not only claiming our legal rights but claiming the natural rights of a child that is begotten in love. No one can hinder us or question our right of approach to our Father.

Satan has Legal Rights over the sinner that God cannot dispute or challenge. He can sell them as slaves; he owns them, body, soul and spirit. But the moment we are born again... receive Eternal Life, the nature of God,—his legal dominion ends.

Christ is the Legal Head of the New Creation, or Family of God, and all the Authority that was given Him, He has given us: (Matthew 28:18), "All authority in heaven," the seat of authority, and "on earth," the place of execution of authority. He is "head over all things," the highest authority in the Universe, for the benefit of the Church which is His body.

THE TWO BABYLONS

COMPLETE AND UNABRIDGED

ALEXANDER HISLOP

The Two Babylons
Alexander Hislop

Fully Illustrated High Res. Images. Complete and Unabridged. Expanded Seventh Edition. This is the first and only seventh edition available in a modern digital edition. Nothing is left out! New material not found in the first six editions!!! Available in eBook and paperback edition exclusively from CrossReach Publications.

"In his work on "The Two Babylons" Dr. Hislop has proven conclusively that all the idolatrous systems of the nations had their origin in what was founded by that mighty Rebel, the beginning of whose kingdom was Babel (Gen. 10:10)."—A. W. Pink, The Antichrist (1923)

There is this great difference between the works of men and the works of God, that the same minute and searching investigation, which displays the defects and imperfections of the one, brings out also the beauties of the other. If the most finely polished needle on which the art of man has been expended be subjected to a microscope, many inequalities, much roughness and clumsiness, will be seen. But if the microscope be brought to bear on the flowers of the field, no such result appears. Instead of their beauty diminishing, new beauties and still more delicate, that have escaped the naked eye, are forthwith discovered; beauties that make us appreciate, in a way which otherwise we could have had little conception of, the full force of the Lord's saying, "Consider the lilies of the field, how they grow; they toil not, neither do they spin: and yet I say unto you, That even Solomon, in all his glory, was not arrayed like one of these." The same law appears also in comparing the Word of God and the most finished productions of men. There are spots and blemishes in the most admired productions of human genius. But the more the Scriptures are searched, the more minutely they are studied, the more their perfection appears; new beauties are brought into light every day; and the discoveries of science, the researches of the learned, and the labours of infidels, all alike conspire to illustrate the wonderful harmony of all the parts, and the Divine beauty that clothes the whole. If this be the case with Scripture in general, it is especially the case with prophetic Scripture. As every spoke in the wheel of Providence revolves, the prophetic symbols start into still more bold and beautiful relief. This is very strikingly the case with the prophetic language that forms the groundwork and corner-stone of the present work. There never has been any difficulty in the mind of any enlightened Protestant in identifying the woman "sitting on seven mountains," and having on her forehead the name written, "Mystery, Babylon the Great," with the Roman apostacy.

Christianity and Liberalism
J. Gresham Machen

The purpose of this book is not to decide the religious issue of the present day, but merely to present the issue as sharply and clearly as possible, in order that the reader may be aided in deciding it for himself. Presenting an issue sharply is indeed by no means a popular business at the present time; there are many who prefer to fight their intellectual battles in what Dr. Francis L. Patton has aptly called a "condition of low visibility." Clear-cut definition of terms in religious matters, bold facing of the logical implications of religious views, is by many persons regarded as an impious proceeding. May it not discourage contribution to mission boards? May it not hinder the progress of consolidation, and produce a poor showing in columns of Church statistics? But with such persons we cannot possibly bring ourselves to agree. Light may seem at times to be an impertinent intruder, but it is always beneficial in the end. The type of religion which rejoices in the pious sound of traditional phrases, regardless of their meanings, or shrinks from "controversial" matters, will never stand amid the shocks of life. In the sphere of religion, as in other spheres, the things about which men are agreed are apt to be the things that are least worth holding; the really important things are the things about which men will fight.

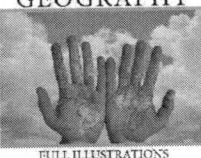

Elementary Geography
Charlotte Mason

This little book is confined to very simple "reading lessons upon the Form and Motions of the Earth, the Points of the Compass, the Meaning of a Map: Definitions."

It is hoped that these reading lessons may afford intelligent teaching, even in the hands of a young teacher.

Children should go through the book twice, and should, after the second reading, be able to answer any of the questions from memory.

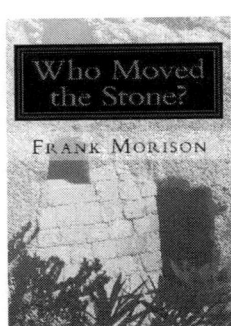

Who Moved the Stone?
Frank Morison

This study is in some ways so unusual and provocative that the writer thinks it desirable to state here very briefly how the book came to take its present form.

In one sense it could have taken no other, for it is essentially a confession, the inner story of a man who originally set out to write one kind of book and found himself compelled by the sheer force of circumstances to write another.

It is not that the facts themselves altered, for they are recorded imperishably in the monuments and in the pages of human history. But the interpretation to be put upon the facts underwent a change. Somehow the perspective shifted—not suddenly, as in a flash of insight or inspiration, but slowly, almost imperceptibly, by the very stubbornness of the facts themselves.

The book as it was originally planned was left high and dry, like those Thames barges when the great river goes out to meet the incoming sea. The writer discovered one day that not only could he no longer write the book as he had once conceived it, but that he would not if he could.

To tell the story of that change, and to give the reasons for it, is the main purpose of the following pages.

The Person and Work of the Holy Spirit
R. A. Torrey

Before one can correctly understand the work of the Holy Spirit, he must first of all know the Spirit Himself. A frequent source of error and fanaticism about the work of the Holy Spirit is the attempt to study and understand His work without first of all coming to know Him as a Person.

It is of the highest importance from the standpoint of worship that we decide whether the Holy Spirit is a Divine Person, worthy to receive our adoration, our faith, our love, and our entire surrender to Himself, or whether it is simply an influence emanating from God or a power or an illumination that God imparts to us. If the Holy Spirit is a person, and a Divine Person, and we do not know Him as such, then we are robbing a Divine Being of the worship and the faith and the love and the surrender to Himself which are His due.

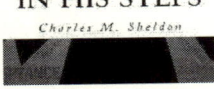

In His Steps
Charles M. Sheldon

The sermon story, In His Steps, or "What Would Jesus Do?" was first written in the winter of 1896, and read by the author, a chapter at a time, to his Sunday evening congregation in the Central Congregational Church, Topeka, Kansas. It was then printed as a serial in The Advance (Chicago), and its reception by the readers of that paper was such that the publishers of The Advance made arrangements for its appearance in book form. It was their desire, in which the author heartily joined, that the story might reach as many readers as possible, hence succeeding editions of paper-covered volumes at a price within the reach of nearly all readers.

The story has been warmly and thoughtfully welcomed by Endeavor societies, temperance organizations, and Y. M. C. A. 's. It is the earnest prayer of the author that the book may go its way with a great blessing to the churches for the quickening of Christian discipleship, and the hastening of the Master's kingdom on earth.

Charles M. Sheldon.
Topeka, Kansas,
November, 1897.

Made in the USA
Middletown, DE
05 May 2024